MY FIRST LEARNING ENGLISH
단어 연습장

Words starting with Aa

• Read and write.

apple
사과

apple

alligator
악어

alligator

airplane
비행기

airplane

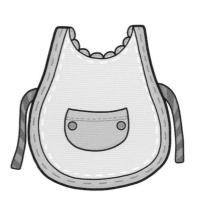

apron
앞치마

apron

ambulance
구급차

ambulance

ant
개미

ant

apple apple

alligator alligator

airplane airplane

apron apron

ambulance ambulance

ant ant

Words starting with **Bb**

● Read and write.

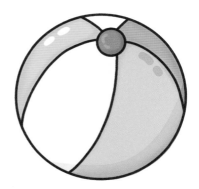

ball
공

ball

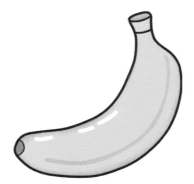

banana
바나나

banana

bear
곰

bear

bus
버스

bus

bag
가방

bag

bird
새

bird

ball ball

banana banana

bear bear

bus bus

bag bag

bird bird

Words starting with Cc

- Read and write.

cat
고양이

car
차

cake
케이크

cat   car   cake

chair
의자

coat
외투

cucumber
오이

chair   coat   cucumber

cat cat

car car

cake cake

chair chair

coat coat

cucumber cucumber

Words starting with **Dd**

● Read and write.

dog
개

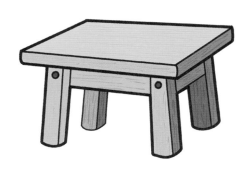

desk
책상

dinosaur
공룡

dog   desk   dinosaur

doctor
의사

donut
도넛

dolphin
돌고래

doctor   donut   dolphin

dog dog

desk desk

dinosaur dinosaur

doctor doctor

donut donut

dolphin dolphin

Words starting with Ee

● Read and write.

egg
달걀

elephant
코끼리

eagle
독수리

egg   elephant   eagle

earth
지구

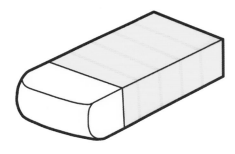

eraser
지우개

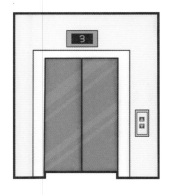

elevator
승강기

earth   eraser   elevator

egg egg

elephant elephant

eagle eagle

earth earth

eraser eraser

elevator elevator

Words starting with

- Read and write.

fish

물고기

flower

꽃

frog

개구리

fish　　　　flower　　　　frog

fork

포크

fox

여우

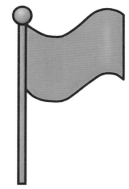

flag

깃발

fork　　　　fox　　　　flag

fish fish

flower flower

frog frog

fork fork

fox fox

flag flag

Words starting with Gg

- Read and write.

goat
염소

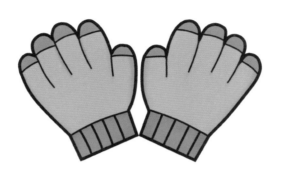

gloves
장갑

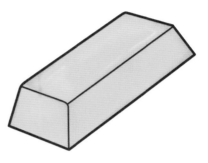

gold
금

goat　　gloves　　gold

grapes
포도

guitar
기타

giraffe
기린

grapes　　guitar　　giraffe

goat goat

gloves gloves

gold gold

grapes grapes

guitar guitar

giraffe giraffe

Words starting with Hh

● Read and write.

helicopter
헬리콥터

house
집

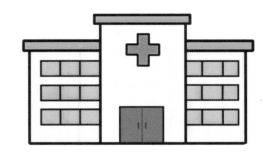

hospital
병원

helicopter   house   hospital

hat
모자

hamburger
햄버거

horse
말

hat   hamburger   horse

helicopter helicopter

house house

hospital hospital

hat hat

hamburger hamburger

horse horse

Words starting with Ii

● Read and write.

ice
얼음

island
섬

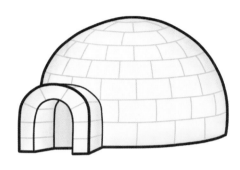

igloo
이글루

ice   island   igloo

iguana
이구아나

ice cream
아이스크림

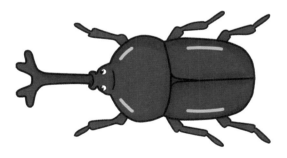

insect
곤충

iguana ice cream insect

ice ice

island island

igloo igloo

iguana iguana

ice cream ice cream

insect insect

Words starting with Jj

● Read and write.

juice
주스

juice

jacket
재킷

jacket

jam
잼

jam

jeep
지프차

jeep

jellyfish
해파리

jellyfish

jaguar
재규어

jaguar

juice juice

jacket jacket

jam jam

jeep jeep

jellyfish jellyfish

jaguar jaguar

Words starting with **Kk**

● Read and write.

kangaroo
캥거루

key
열쇠

kite
연

kangaroo   key   kite

king
왕

koala
코알라

knife
칼

king   koala   knife

kangaroo kangaroo

key key

kite kite

king king

koala koala

knife knife

Words starting with

- Read and write.

lamp
램프

lion
사자

ladder
사다리

lamp   lion   ladder

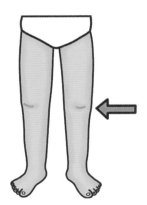

lemon
레몬

leg
다리

ladybug
무당벌레

lemon   leg   ladybug

lamp lamp

lion lion

ladder ladder

lemon lemon

leg leg

ladybug ladybug

Words starting with Mm

• Read and write.

moon
달

monkey
원숭이

mountain
산

moon   monkey   mountain

map
지도

mushroom
버섯

milk
우유

map   mushroom   milk

moon moon

monkey monkey

mountain mountain

map map

mushroom mushroom

milk milk

Words starting with **Nn**

● Read and write.

nest
둥지

noodle
국수

necklace
목걸이

nest   noodle   necklace

nurse
간호사

notebook
공책

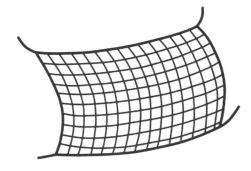

net
그물

nurse   notebook   net

nest nest

noodle noodle

necklace necklace

nurse nurse

notebook notebook

net net

Words starting with Oo

• Read and write.

orange   **o**wl   **o**tter

오렌지   올빼미   수달

orange   owl   otter

 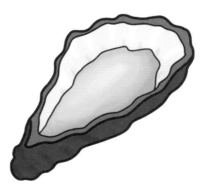 

onion   **o**yster   **o**ctopus

양파   굴   문어

onion   oyster   octopus

orange   orange

owl   owl

oyster   oyster

onion   onion

octopus   octopus

otter   otter

Words starting with

● Read and write.

 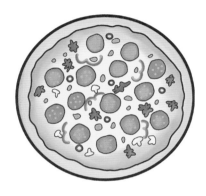 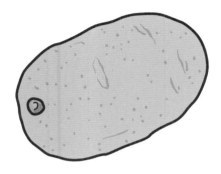

pencil   **p**izza   **p**otato

연필   피자   감자

pencil   pizza   potato

panda   **p**rincess   **p**iano

판다   공주   피아노

panda   princess   piano

pencil pencil

pizza pizza

potato potato

panda panda

princess princess

piano piano

Words starting with Qq

● Read and write.

queen
여왕

question
질문

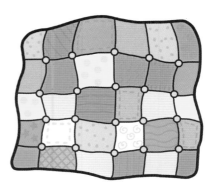

quilt
누비이불

queen   question   quilt

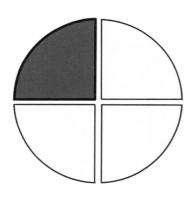

quarter
4분의 1

quail
메추라기

quiz
퀴즈

quarter   quail   quiz

queen queen

question question

quilt quilt

quarter quarter

quail quail

quiz quiz

Words starting with **Rr**

• Read and write.

rabbit

토끼

rabbit

rain

비

rain

rose

장미

rose

robot

로봇

robot

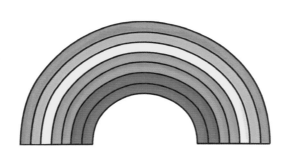

rainbow

무지개

rainbow

rice

쌀

rice

rabbit rabbit

rain rain

rose rose

robot robot

rainbow rainbow

rice rice

Words starting with **Ss**

● Read and write.

sun

해

sun

sweater

스웨터

sweater

star

별

star

socks

양말

socks

strawberry

딸기

strawberry

sheep

양

sheep

sun sun

sweater sweater

star star

socks socks

strawberry strawberry

sheep sheep

Words starting with T t

• Read and write.

table
식탁

table

tree
나무

tree

truck
트럭

truck

tomato
토마토

tomato

train
기차

train

tiger
호랑이

tiger

table table

tree tree

truck truck

tomato tomato

train train

tiger tiger

Words starting with **Uu**

• Read and write.

umbrella
우산

unicorn
유니콘

uniform
유니폼

umbrella   unicorn   uniform

uncle
삼촌

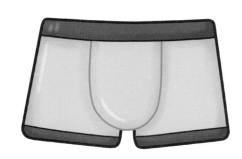

underwear
속옷

unicycle
외발 자전거

uncle   underwear   unicycle

umbrella umbrella

unicorn unicorn

uniform uniform

uncle uncle

underwear underwear

unicycle unicycle

Vv ALPHABET

Words starting with Vv

- Read and write.

van

승합차

v a n

volcano

화산

volcano

violin

바이올린

violin

vest

조끼

vest

vegetable

채소

vegetable

vet

수의사

vet

van van

volcano volcano

violin violin

vest vest

vegetable vegetable

vet vet

Words starting with **Ww**

- Read and write.

water

물

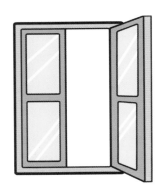

window

창문

wheel

바퀴

water　　window　　wheel

whale

고래

watermelon

수박

wolf

늑대

whale　　watermelon　　wolf

water water

window window

wheel wheel

whale whale

watermelon watermelon

wolf wolf

Words starting with

- Read and write.

x-ray
엑스레이

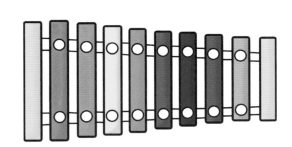
xylophone
실로폰

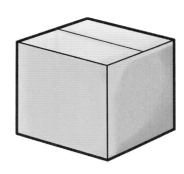
box
상자

x-ray   xylophone   box

taxi
택시

Xmas
크리스마스

ax
도끼

taxi   Xmas   ax

x-ray x-ray

xylophone xylophone

box box

taxi taxi

Xmas Xmas

ax ax

Words starting with Yy

● Read and write.

yogurt
요구르트

yacht
요트

yarn
털실

yogurt   yacht   yarn

yawn
하품

yo-yo
요요

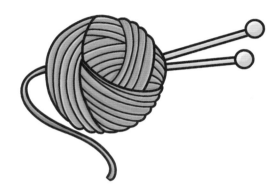

yak
들소

yawn   yo-yo   yak

yogurt yogurt

yacht yacht

yarn yarn

yawn yawn

yo-yo yo-yo

yak yak

Words starting with **Zz**

- Read and write.

zebra

얼룩말

zoo

동물원

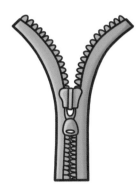

zipper

지퍼

zebra   zoo   zipper

zigzag

지그재그

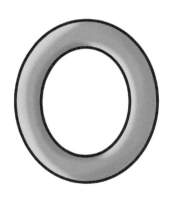

zero

0, 제로

zoo keeper

동물원 사육사

zigzag   zero   zoo keeper

zebra zebra

zoo zoo

zipper zipper

zigzag zigzag

zero zero

zoo keeper zoo keeper

English words

Aa
 apple alligator airplane apron ambulance ant

Bb
 ball banana bear bus bag bird

Cc
 cat car cake  chair  coat cucumber

Dd
 dog desk dinosaur doctor donut dolphin

Ee
 egg elephant eagle earth eraser elevator

Ff
 fish flower frog  fork  fox flag

Gg
 goat gloves gold grapes guitar giraffe

Hh
 helicopter house hospital hat  hamburger horse

Ii
 ice island igloo iguana ice cream insect

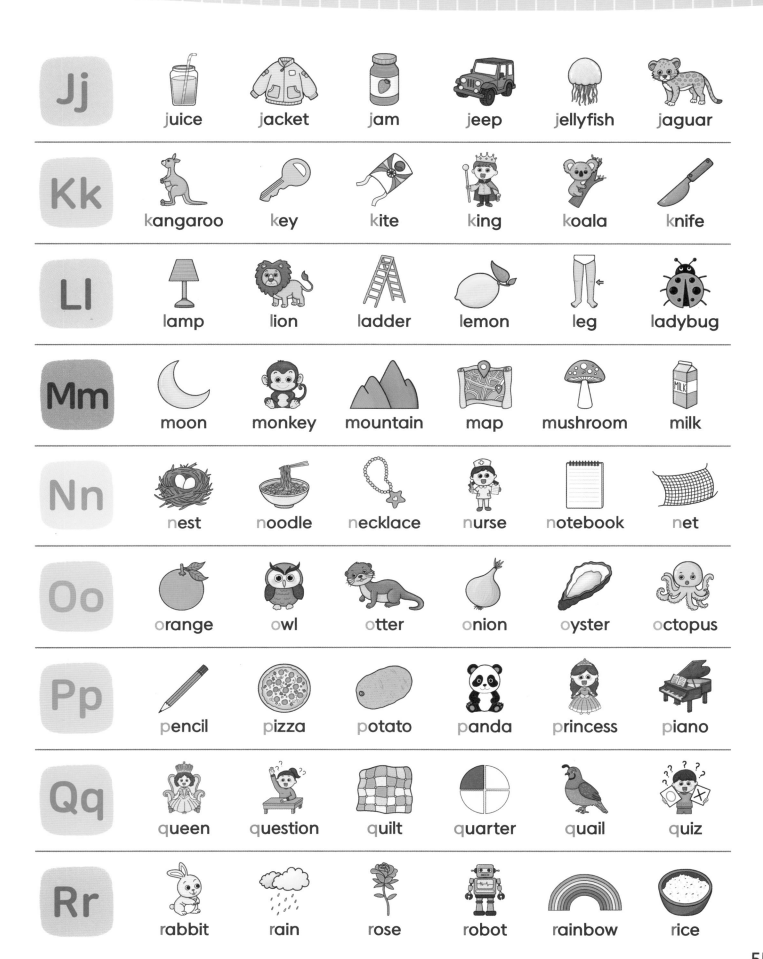

Jj	juice	jacket	jam	jeep	jellyfish	jaguar
Kk	kangaroo	key	kite	king	koala	knife
Ll	lamp	lion	ladder	lemon	leg	ladybug
Mm	moon	monkey	mountain	map	mushroom	milk
Nn	nest	noodle	necklace	nurse	notebook	net
Oo	orange	owl	otter	onion	oyster	octopus
Pp	pencil	pizza	potato	panda	princess	piano
Qq	queen	question	quilt	quarter	quail	quiz
Rr	rabbit	rain	rose	robot	rainbow	rice

Ss	sun	sweater	star	socks	strawberry
					sheep

Ss
 sun   sweater   star   socks   strawberry   sheep

Tt
 table   tree   truck   tomato   train   tiger

Uu
 umbrella   unicorn   uniform   uncle   underwear   unicycle

Vv
 van   volcano   violin   vest   vegetable   vet

Ww
 water   window   wheel   whale    watermelon   wolf

Xx
 x-ray   xylophone   box   taxi   Xmas   ax

Yy
 yogurt   yacht   yarn   yawn   yo-yo   yak

Zz
 zebra   zoo   zipper   zigzag   zero   zoo keeper